P9-DYZ-800

A NEW ENGLAND TOWN

IN EARLY PHOTOGRAPHS

149 Illustrations of Southbridge, Massachusetts, 1878-1930

SELECTED AND EDITED BY EDMUND V. GILLON, JR.

INTRODUCTION AND CAPTIONS BY ARTHUR J. KAVANAGH

Dover Publications, Inc., New York

Visual Studies Workshop
Research Center
Rochester, N.Y.

Copyright © 1976 by Dover Publications, Inc.
All rights reserved under Pan American and International
Copyright Conventions.

Published in Canada by General Publishing Company, Ltd.,
30 Lesmill Road, Don Mills, Toronto, Ontario.
Published in the United Kingdom by Constable and Company,
Ltd., 10 Orange Street, London WC 2.

*A New England Town in Early Photographs: 149 Illustrations
of Southbridge, Massachusetts, 1878–1930* is a new work,
first published by Dover Publications, Inc., in 1976.

International Standard Book Number: 0–486–23286–7
Library of Congress Catalog Card Number: 75–46384 9-78 14

Manufactured in the United States of America
Dover Publications, Inc.
180 Varick Street, New York, N.Y. 10014

Title page: Composite photo of Main Street, looking northwest, about 1880. Dwelling houses, some converted to business use, still stood among the business blocks. The wooden buildings on the extreme left were replaced a dozen years later by the new Y. The building with the "Boston Branch" sign later was known as the Blanchard block. The Universalist Church is just to the right of center. At the extreme right is Hartwell's drugstore. The wooden structures around the trunks of the small trees were put there to keep horses from gnawing the bark.

Front cover. A crowd gathered on Main Street for a celebration, around the turn of the century.

Rear cover. A view of Main Street in 1916 during the centennial celebration of the town's incorporation.

To my parents
EDMUND AND ETHEL GILLON,
residents of Southbridge for nearly half a century.

Southeastern view of the central part of Southbridge
(nineteenth-century woodcut).

Following page: Assembling for a parade, in front of
the Dresser House, 1887. The police force is in the
front line. The clock in the Baptist steeple is the
official town clock. The town hall is on a side street,
and the town long ago decided to put the clock where
it would be most visible.

INTRODUCTION

This book is a portrait of a New England town in the period from the 1870s to about 1930. The town is Southbridge, in the south central part of Massachusetts.

Like most communities, Southbridge has its own individuality. However, because people are much alike everywhere, many things about it are reminiscent of other places. The picture of "Dom" Pocai's peanut stand may make older residents of a certain Vermont city think of Billy Lambkin's popcorn and ice cream wagon, which used to be drawn up beside the park on Sunday evenings during the band concerts. The scenes of parades may lead people in a city in Maine to recall parades in their own town and then to think of Eddie Emmons, who took great delight in leading parades and built up a large collection of magnificent uniforms for that sole purpose. To a considerable extent a portrait of Southbridge is also a portrait of other towns and cities.

Compared to other places in New England, Southbridge is a fairly young town. It was not incorporated until after the War of 1812–14.

Although the occupation of nearby towns had begun somewhat earlier, settlement of this area did not begin until about a century after the founding of Boston. By that time the towns near the sea coast were becoming overpopulated, and it was increasingly difficult to find adequate land for farming for the younger generations as they grew up. As a result there was a movement toward unoccupied lands in the interior, some of which had previously been considered unattractive. In 1730 a group of people, mostly from Medfield, began to move into a grant which had been given them by the Massachusetts General Court and which lay between the older grants for Oxford and Brimfield. At about the same time settlers began to come into the previously unoccupied adjacent portion of the Oxford grant.

Danger of Indian attacks in this part of the province was long past, but each settler was faced with the task of felling the trees and clearing his fields, and erecting buildings to shelter his family, his livestock and his crops. The cave where James Denison spent part of his first winter here is well known, and descendants of William McKinstry can point out the open spot on which he spent his first night in the area, and the dugout he shared with another man while they were making their start.

For about eighty years the principal source of livelihood was farming. What the inhabitants lived in, what they ate and what they wore were mainly the products of their own woodlots and farms and of their own direct labor. The few mills that were established— a couple of sawmills, a couple of grist mills, a mill for making linseed oil and a couple of clothier's mills— were for processing the farmers' products. (The clothier's mills, which required water power, were for the purpose of fulling and finishing the homemade woolens, tasks which most housewives did not have the strength or facilities to do themselves.)

During this period the number of farms and the number of inhabitants increased, and some political changes took place. The Medfield grant was incorporated as the town of Sturbridge. The western part of Oxford was divided up, and from the parts and some previously unincorporated land the towns of Dudley and Charlton were formed. On the national scene the Revolutionary War came and went, and the Constitution and the Bill of Rights were adopted.

In the mid-1790s people in the southeastern part of Sturbridge and the adjacent parts of Dudley and Charlton, who lived far from the centers and churches of their respective towns, began action toward becoming incorporated as a separate town of their own. Because of opposition from the older communities the

The most thickly settled part of town, seen from a hill to the south, about 1880. Globe Village is at the left. Centre Village at the center and right. Sandersdale is out of sight to the right. The Congregational Church is to the right of center, and the building next to it, with the smaller tower, is the town hall. Near the center of the right-hand page is the Baptist steeple, clock and all. The town hall was built in the late 1830s, mainly with Southbridge's share of Federal money returned to the states. It seems that in 1836 the Federal government had a surplus in the treasury!

Looking east on Main Street from in front of the Universalist Church, probably about 1910. The trees in the roadway gave a pleasant shade. In those days it was safe for the photographer to set up his tripod in the middle of the road. And it didn't make much difference whether one drove on the right or on the left.

process took longer than they had expected, and it was not until 1816 that they achieved their goal. They chose the name Southbridge.

During the period of the struggle for incorporation a development began which would change the town from a simple farming community into the Southbridge shown in the following pages. This innovation was the introduction of the mechanical spinning of yarn and the weaving of cloth, the beginning of the textile industry. The first successful mills for this purpose had been set up in the area of Providence, Rhode Island, around 1790. Within a few years there was a rush for similar developments wherever there was a good source of power.

In those days a good source of power meant, for all practical purposes, water power. The Quinebaug River, flowing from west to east through the proposed town, had several good sites, two of which were already occupied by the small mills mentioned above. These were attractive to persons, both local residents and people from other places, who wished to embark on the new manufacturing.

By 1816, the year the town was incorporated, manufacturing operations were under way at three places along the river. The farthest upstream was at a site already occupied by one of the saw and grist mills and the linseed-oil mill. Here in 1814 was incorporated the Globe Manufacturing Company. Although this company soon gave way to successors and passed out of existence in 1819, the part of town in which it was located is still known as Globe Village, or simply the Globe. The largest textile manufacturing complex grew up in this area.

Farther down stream, around the water power of the earliest saw mill and grist mill, another factory center developed. It was near these mills that the first meeting house had been built at the beginning of the efforts toward incorporation of the town. The area was known as the Centre Village. As the town grew the main business district came to be located in the Centre Village.

Between these locations another site was occupied by a mill in 1814 and for a number of years thereafter.

In the years following the incorporation two more sites were developed extensively. In 1821 a dam and mill were built about three quarters of a mile down-stream from the dam at the Centre Village. Later, in the 1880s, after two mills on the spot had been destroyed by fire, the property was taken over by the town's leading manufacturer of spectacles. The optical manufacturing business was then emerging as one of the town's important industries.

In 1834–35 a dam and mill were constructed at a fifth site, about a mile below the preceding one. Later the property came into the ownership of a man named James Sanders. That part of town and the extensive mills that developed there have ever since been known as Sandersdale.

The Centre Village mill site and the one just above and the one just below it are in the part of town which was taken from Charlton. A few historically minded citizens of Charlton can be found even today who mourn: "When Southbridge was incorporated they took all our best water power!" Certainly these sites were an important factor in the growth of Southbridge.

As the business of the mills grew, the countryside was not able to provide enough workers. Over the years the supply, mostly unskilled initially, consisted to a great extent of Irish and French-Canadian immigrants, and later of Italians, Poles and others. It is largely to their influx that the town owes its population growth. Their coming changed Southbridge from a community of farmers of English and Scotch-Irish descent, solidly Protestant, into a busy town with a majority of people of other origins and other customs, and of Roman Catholic and later of Eastern Orthodox religion. The history of Southbridge is in large part the history of all these people's learning in some fashion to live with each other. Many New England towns and cities went through a similar experience.

The Irish were the first to arrive in very great numbers. When the first Catholic Mass was said in Southbridge in 1840, it was attended by twelve persons. Seven were Irish and the rest were Germans and French Canadians. As late as 1867 the Catholic parish consisted about equally of Irish and of French.

The French Canadians have been by far the largest population group. Although some were here earlier, the great migration began after the Civil War. In 1852, when the total population was about 3000 (it had been 830 when the town was incorporated), a church census showed 322 French. In 1860 the population was 4131 and there were only 510 French. In 1887, when the population was about 6100, the number of French had jumped to 3380. By 1900 the population had reached 10,000, and the number of French slightly exceeded 6000.

It was during the 1880s that the editor of one of the two local newspapers, responding to complaints that a place the size of Southbridge should have a better paper, lamented that over half the population could not read English and hence had no interest in an English-language newspaper. (This editor, one of the town's better ones, adopted for a time the policy of printing some French-language items written by members of the French community. This greatly pleased the French people and improved the circulation of the paper.)

By 1919, the year in which Felix Gatineau published his *Histoire des Franco-Américains de Southbridge, Massachusetts*, not only a majority of the population, but also a majority of the registered voters, were French-Canadian. In his introduction Mr. Gatineau said (in French of course), "the Canadians of Southbridge . . . have the controlling hand in the affairs of the town and impose their will everywhere. Southbridge indeed is a little corner of the Province of Quebec. . . ."

It was only after 1900 that Italians, Poles, Greeks and Albanians began to come in considerable numbers.

The mixing of all these groups was naturally accompanied by friction. People already in town looked down on and resented newcomers with a different language and different customs. After the newcomers became settled they and their children in turn looked down on and resented later comers. One man of Polish descent recalls that his father, who in 1913 was one of the first Poles to come to town, told him that at that time the Polish fellows didn't go out alone in the evening but rather in groups of two or three, because otherwise the French fellows would "jump" them. In a way this was history repeating itself, because many years before it had been the French fellows who didn't go out alone, lest they be jumped by the Irish.

As time went by, and as the younger generations grew up, some of the old feelings abated. People became accustomed to working and associating with each other. The young folks began to forsake the old ways. There were intermarriages, usually against the opposition, and to the anguish, of the old folks on both sides. The old dividing lines still existed, but they became increasingly blurred.

Most of the newcomers came without special skills and entered the mills as common laborers. Some in time advanced to more important positions. Others went into business, with stores, blacksmith shops, harness shops and even factories of their own. Many of their children and grandchildren went on to higher education and became clergymen, doctors and lawyers. Their success was a fulfillment of what has been called the American dream. Of course there were also a great many who did not succeed in this fashion.

While the town was developing as a small manufacturing center, the life of the farms still went on. The family shown in the picture on page 105, who were descendants of the original settler on the farm, happened to live in Charlton, but there were at least three families in Southbridge at the time who were also living on farms which had been settled by their forebears, and there were other farmers not living on the ancestral lands whose families had been in the area since the early days. Many of the descendants of the old families went to work in the mills, but some of the newcomers and their descendants went into farming.

The period covered by the book was one of great changes in ways of living.

By 1870 gas lighting had already come to the more thickly settled parts of town, but most people still relied on oil lamps and candles. The railroad had come in 1866, but otherwise people had to rely on horse-power or "shank's mare" for transportation. (On one occasion, when an epidemic of illness had struck down most of the horses, the selectmen made an inspection tour of some sort on a wagon drawn by a pair of oxen. Oxen, though powerful, are slow-moving, and it must have been a very leisurely trip.)

Electric lighting began to be introduced in the 1880s, again only in the more thickly settled parts.

Telephones also began to come in the 1880s. The first installation consisted of three phones. The newspaper editor mentioned above was one of the movers in forming the telephone company. One of the phones was in the newspaper office in the Centre Village and another was in a store at the Globe. He published an

"Dom" Pocai outside his peanut stand, next to Brouso's harness shop.
His peanuts were famous for miles around.

article describing the first use of the instruments. The tryout was witnessed by several interested persons in both places, and the article said that speech and even music were transmitted clearly over the line.

Trolley cars first ran in 1897. (Southbridge never had horsecars, though they had been proposed.) The line of the Southbridge & Sturbridge Street Railway ran from Sandersdale through Centre Village and the Globe and as far as the village of Fiskdale in Sturbridge. On the way it passed the Sturbridge Fairgrounds (and also the present site of Old Sturbridge Village). In 1902 the line became part of an interurban system ultimately running from Worcester to Springfield. Relatively easy access to these places, especially to Worcester, was thus provided.

The trolley cars were an important part of the life of the town until automobiles became common. They sometimes served purposes not strictly utilitarian. For a time saloons were legally closed in Southbridge, but open in Sturbridge. It became quite common to ride to Fiskdale in the evening, patronize the establishments there, then rush for the last car back to Southbridge. Sometimes the motorman himself was so unsteady that he let somebody else run the car.

By the late 1920s the business of the line had decreased so much that it was shut down. It was replaced by a line of busses.

Readers who hope to find this a book of pictures of a lovely village green with a white steeple soaring above the treetops, elegant mansions like those of Wiscasset and avenues like North and South Streets in Litchfield, will be disappointed. Southbridge never did have that sort of village green. The lovely mansions and the wide avenues are the places where a few of the rich folks lived; not all even of Wiscasset or Litchfield is like that.

Those who like to see people and their children and the places where they lived and worked and played half a century to a century ago may find much to interest them.

ARTHUR J. KAVANAGH

A NEW ENGLAND TOWN

IN

EARLY PHOTOGRAPHS

Following four pages: Two panoramic views, the first published in 1878, the second in 1892. The directions of view are different in the two. In the first, the observer looks from south to north, so that the Centre Village is to his right and the Globe (Globe Village) to his left. For many years there was a strong rivalry between the two villages, and an imaginary boundary was drawn between them on the crest of the hill between Marcy and Cross Streets and along South Street. An old source states: "The boys were as partisan as their elders. The Glober was despised by the Towner, while the latter, if he had occasion to visit 'Butts Green' or 'Canada Hill,' often returned home with the marks of a too zealous Glober plainly imprinted on his person."

The second view shows much the same part of town, but seen from the north. The Centre Village, with most of the stores and churches, is at the left. Globe Village, containing the Hamilton Woolen Company's extensive complex of factories, is at the right.

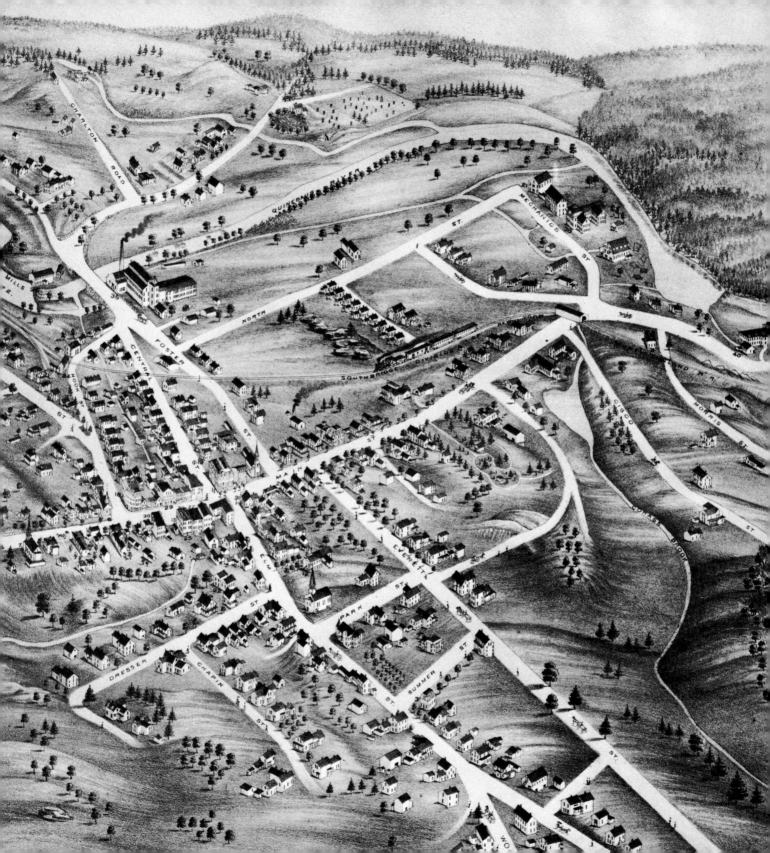

Above, and following four pages: A composite picture of the north side of Main Street, about 1918. The building at the left is the Whitford Block, at the corner of Main and Hamilton Streets. Next is the Phelps Theatre building. The Hotel Columbia was built in the first decade of this century. The building housing Samuel Williams' Furniture Warehouse had once been the home of C. E. Ellis' store. Names on some of the next six establishments appear in other pictures in the book. Hartwell's drugstore stands on the left corner of Central Street. Looking down that street, on the left are the building where the Salvation Army had rooms, and the old firehouse;

on the right a bit of the Central House can be seen. The large
building on the right-hand corner was built in 1871–2 as the
Dresser House, a hotel, with stores on the ground floor. The
Boston Branch Store was in a low, wooden building. The
structure on the right is the Ammidown Block, built at about
the same time as the Dresser House. For about forty years
its owner gave the town a rent-free lease of the second floor
for a library. The Baptist Church is out of sight to the right.
Except for the recent loss of the former Dresser House and the
adjacent building by fire, this side of Main Street looks much
the same today.

Following pages: Detail from preceding panorama. The coming of the movies brought entertainment to town every day, and "going to the show" became a part of the life of many people, especially the children. The Ford parked in front of the building had a brass band around the radiator.

Above, and following six pages: A composite view of the south side of Main Street, about 1918. The YMCA building, erected in 1893, is at the left. Looking up Elm Street, on the left is Felix Gatineau's store and on the right is the tower of the present fire station. The Blanchard Block, built in 1860 as the Edwards House, a hotel, is on the right-hand corner. The Edwards Company occupied the tall building and half of the lower one. The Plaza Theatre is in the old Dresser Opera

House. (In a small town, any building having a large hall suitable for meetings and entertainments might be dignified with the appellation of opera house.) The Southbridge Herald building was erected in 1878. The title page panorama shows a small cottage standing in the place here occupied by the St. Onge store and the end of Chapin Street. The buildings to the right of the Woolworth store show a stage in the gradual change from residential to business district.

28

Above: The handwritten title on the back of the original photo says, "John W. Silk Saloon," 1889. This was in the Globe.

Opposite: Joe Bourke's music store, 1889. This emporium was located on Hamilton Street, just behind the Universalist Church.

Above: The various branches of the Blanchard family, whose members appear several times in this book, were engaged in a multitude of affairs. Since most of the pictures of stores were formal photographs and not mere snapshots, the proprietor and the clerks usually posed, as well as anyone else who happened to be around. This shot dates from 1889.

Opposite: Grocery store. Crackers and cookies were sold by the pound, weighed out by the clerk from glass-covered boxes like those at the left. Interior pictures like this one were taken with light from burning flash powder. The photographer poured magnesium powder into a little trough, held the trough above his head, cautioned everybody not to move, opened the camera lens and touched off the powder. The powder burned almost with a small explosion. The photographer quickly closed the lens, and a cloud of white magnesium ash spread through the air and settled down onto everything.

36

Opposite: One of the former residences on Main Street converted to business use, about 1898. The three women are the ones who conducted "Dress Making Up Stairs." Note the fashion sheets in the upper window, perhaps cut from a fashion magazine.

Below: Joe Bebo, about 1898, whose liquor store at 5 Central Street appears on page 53, later moved down to number 17, formerly occupied by F. LaRiviere (pages 80–81). Bebo is the bearded man standing near the horse. The name on the wagon is evidently that of a brewing company he represented. The reason for the celebration is not known.

Above: Holden's grocery store on Main Street, 1889. The display is partly obscured by reflections from the window panes. One poster advertises the circus on July 8 and 9.
Opposite: "Dom" Pocai in 1889, some years before the picture on page 11 was taken.

Opposite: Brouso's harness shop, on Main Street, 1889. Harness makers were as necessary then as garage men are now.

Following pages: Felix Gatineau's grocery store on Elm Street. The owner is standing at the left. He was a leader in the French community, author of the *Histoire des Franco-Américains de Southbridge,* and active in politics. For a time he represented the town in the state legislature. After his death a statue of him was erected at the corner of Main and South Streets. This statue is commonly referred to as "Felix." A few trade names still current can be seen in the picture.

Below: Felix Gatineau on a delivery sleigh, about 1885, before he had his own store. His wife and little daughter are on the porch.

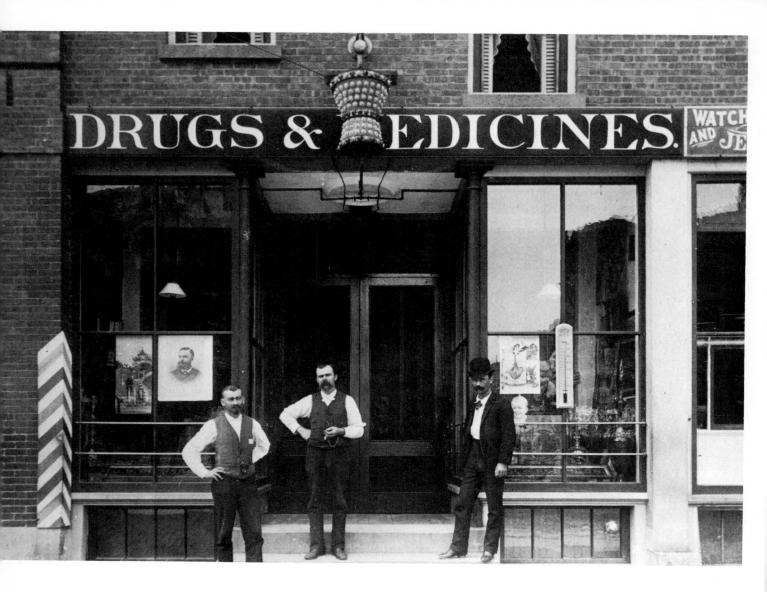

J. W. Robinson's drugstore at the corner of Main and Elm in 1889.

Ellis' grocery store, a rather high-class establishment. "Grain" was feed for horses, cattle and poultry. Many families not primarily engaged in farming kept a horse, a cow or a few hens.

Below: Adelard LaPorte's grocery store in the Globe, showing the delivery force, about 1918. The two covered sleds at the right carried meat, which was sold from door to door. The drivers were loaded up and ready to start at 6:00 A.M. While selling the meat, they took orders for groceries. Then they made a second trip to deliver the groceries. The boy in the white apron on the steps was about 14 years old. During the influenza epidemic of 1918 only he and the owner were not sick, and he was sent out alone to cover the two meat routes. He started off with a horse that knew one route well. When it stopped in front of a house he would go in, ask if the family was one of LaPorte's customers, and sell meat or take orders. He went over one route this way, then hitched in the horse that knew the other route, and went over that one in the same way.

Opposite: An 1889 picture of the Delehanty furniture store, which is still doing business in the same building in the Globe. The toy wagons, including the wheels, were made of wood, just as real wagons were. The iron horse's head in the foreground is the top of a hitching post.

Above: Schomburg's cigar store, probably about 1900. Not all cigar-store figures were Indians. This one was called "the Dutchman." Many years later, after changes in the ownership of the store, the Dutchman ended up in the garage of the mother of a former owner. This lady was planning to have him taken to the dump when a stranger appeared at her door and inquired about a cigar-store image he had heard she had. He said he would like to buy it. The lady, a canny Scotswoman, said she did have one, but some people had been interested in it, and she did not think she ought to let it go. After some discussion the man offered her $800. She decided she could sell it for that amount.

Opposite: "Hub" Dresser's cigar store and pool room. Dresser, on the right, had a reputation as a practical joker.

Above: The Salvation Army occupied rooms over Joe Bebo's saloon, a little way up Central Street from the fire and police station. The cigar store at the right had an attraction called "box ball," a sort of bowling game played on an alley about three feet wide and twenty feet long, with paddles instead of pins. The price was five cents a string. A player who got a spare got a free cigar or a chance to roll another string.

Opposite: Dry-goods store, 1889. This picture was taken before the YMCA building was erected, and the Y occupied rooms over the store. In the left foreground is the public drinking fountain, which has been described as "an unsightly pagoda-like affair, surmounted by an iron pole on top of which were twin lights. Two battered and rusty tin cups hung on long chains."

Following pages: The men's clothing and shoe department of the Edwards Company store, a Southbridge institution for over a century. It was started as a dry-goods store by John Edwards in the mid-1800's. Over the years the ownership changed, and it was known successively as Carpenter, Irwin and Company; Carpenter and Company; Paige, Carpenter and Company; and the Johnson, Colburn Company. At about the time of this picture (taken around 1912) the name was changed to the Edwards Company. These various names can be seen on the store building in views of Main Street over the years. The archway at the left rear opens into the women's department. The manager is behind the counter.

53

Above: Joseph Serleto's fruit and vegetable store on Elm Street. The building reflected in the window is the Blanchard block.

Opposite: The yard-goods section of the women's department of the Edwards Company store about 1912. In this picture the manager is standing at the right behind the radiator. The apparatus over the head of the woman clerk carried money and sales slips to a cashier in a booth at the rear of the room. Several of the carriers were located about the store, each connected to the booth by a steel wire. Money and sales slip were placed in the cylindrical container, the clerk pulled on the wooden handle, and the container shot along the wire to the cashier. Change was returned in the same manner. This was an early labor-saving device in storekeeping.

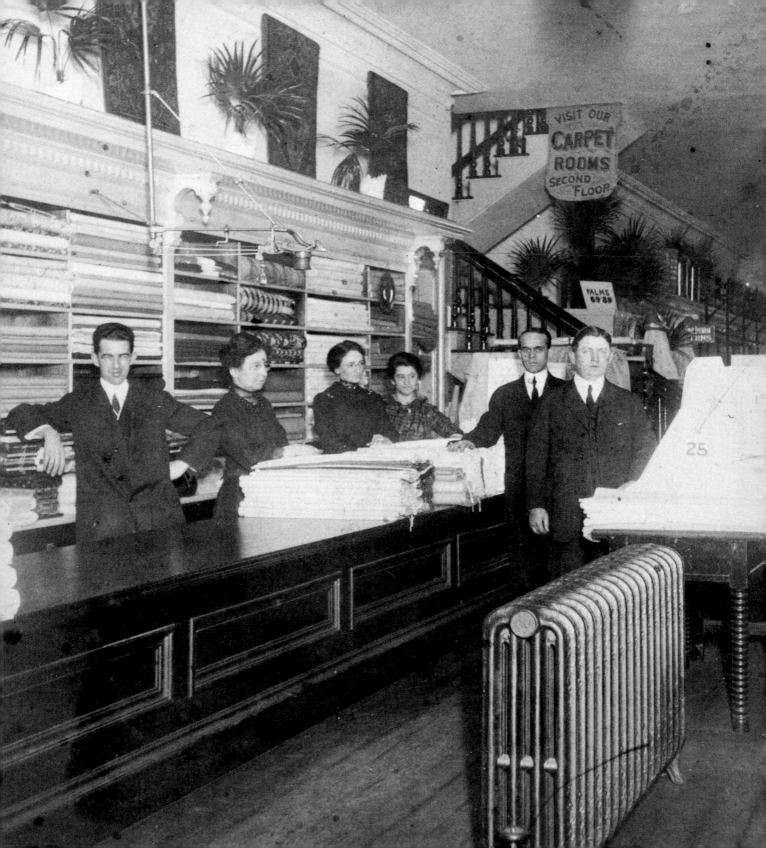

Opposite: Front view of the Edwards Company's department store, about 1930. It extended into the building on the right, which contained the men's department. A staircase built into the Blanchard building on the left was used to give access to Edwards Hall, a ballroom, on the third floor. The store had some claim to being considered the oldest department store in the nation.

Below: The Edwards Company (circa 1930) shows what the well-dressed man will wear.

Above: Lenti's shoe-repair shop on Elm Street. The long stove pipe gave extra radiating surface and helped to heat the room. *Opposite:* Interior of Julian Gabree's hardware store in the Ammidown (library) block, about 1930. The store front can be seen in the picture on page 72.

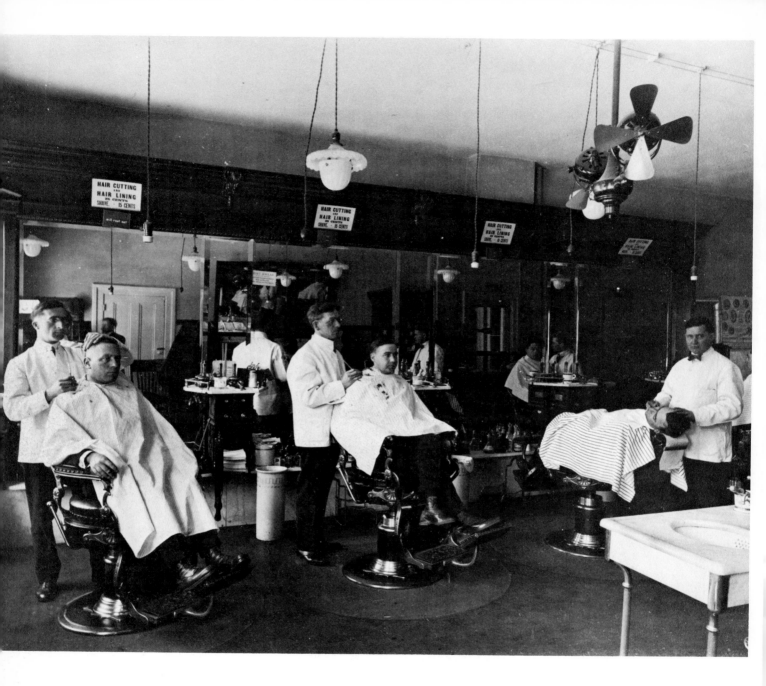

John Adam's barber shop on Main Street. Many men went to
the barber shop regularly to be shaved. Lathering was done
with brush, mug and cake soap. Against the back wall, visible
in the mirror, is a cabinet containing individual mugs and
brushes for fastidious customers who wished to provide them.
Most such mugs bore the owner's name in gold letters.

Right: Another barber shop, a small one, 1889. This was on Hamilton Street, half way from the Centre to the Globe. The proprietor combined barbering with tobacco selling.

Below: Men's store, 1895. The older men prefer the old-style collars and ties. The young fellow has the snappy bow tie. Vests are de rigueur.

Above: Bar of the Nipmuck House.
Opposite: The Nipmuck House, a boarding house on Central Street. The bar was in the basement. The proprietor is standing on the porch.

65

Above: Valdivia's tobacco store, 1889.
Opposite: Another bar, possibly Joseph Bebo's.

Above: Main Street about 1890. The boy in the foreground apparently ran around during the long film exposure necessary at the time.
Opposite: Lobby of the Central House.

Above: The bar of the Central House.

Opposite: The Central House on Central Street across from the fire station. The street light hanging from the arm attached to the pole is a carbon-arc lamp. The carbons in these lamps gradually burned away as the lamp operated. Periodically a man from the light company would come around, lower the lamp by means of the small windlass attached to the pole, replace the carbons and raise the lamp back into place. The stumps of the old carbons were often picked up and treasured by children. They were valuable for marking on rocks and foundation walls or, where there were concrete sidewalks, for marking out squares for playing hopscotch.

Above: Main Street looking northwest in 1917, showing much of the central business district. The stone-fronted building at the left houses the two banks. The building next to it, with the small conical tower, is the YMCA (an unusually large Y for a town of this size). Then comes the Blanchard block, shown in a picture on page 150 after a disastrous fire. Next is the Edwards block. At right center the steeple of the recently erected Notre Dame Church, pride of the French community, shows against the sky. Near it can be seen portions of the much older Universalist and Methodist steeples. The building in front of Notre Dame is the Hartwell block, at the corner of Central Street. Next (moving right) is the Masonic Building, which had been built in 1871 as the Dresser House, a hotel. The Ammidown block, at the extreme right, had been built at about the same time, partly as a business venture and partly to house the town library, which occupied rent-free quarters there for many years. The auto was well on its way toward displacing the horse; there seem to be only two horse-drawn vehicles on the street. The pavement was made of creosoted wooden blocks. When wet they were very slippery.

Opposite: The Hartwell block, about 1898. This building was put up in the 1860s. It has always housed a drugstore which, despite changes in ownership, has always been called Hartwell's. When the interurban streetcar line was being built, the crew, despite protests, insisted on putting one of the poles too near the door of the drugstore. Thereupon one of the selectmen, a direct-acting Irishman, appeared with his axe and chopped the pole down. The replacement was put in a different spot.

Opposite: Buildings decorated for the town's Centennial celebration in 1916.
Below: It was fun to walk beside the band—a parade in 1898.

Left: Main Street, seen from an upper window of the YMCA, about 1920. "Back-in" parking was then the rule. Some of the cars are equipped with Boyce Moto-Meters. These were thermometers, mounted so as to replace the radiator cap, to permit the driver to see whether his engine was overheating while driving.

Opposite: The parade of the Centennial celebration in 1916.

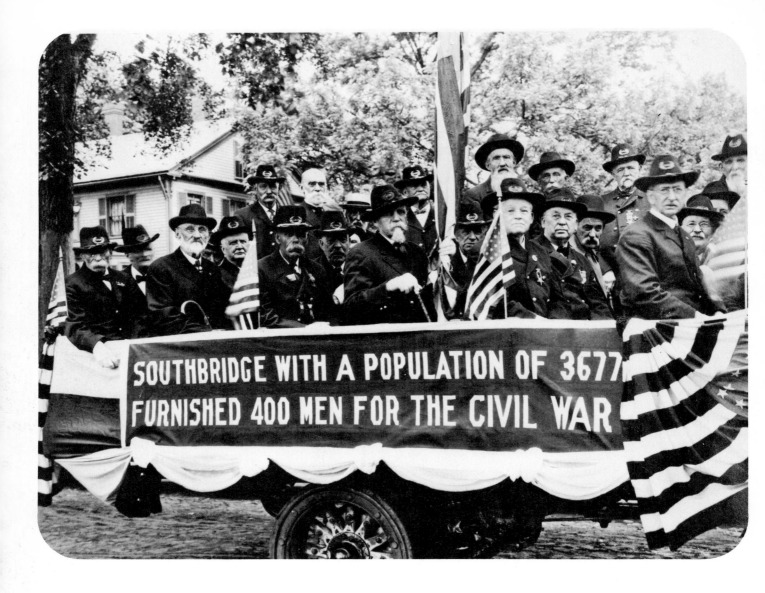

SOUTHBRIDGE WITH A POPULATION OF 3677
FURNISHED 400 MEN FOR THE CIVIL WAR

Above: The Grand Army of the Republic, veterans of the Civil War, in the parade at the Centennial celebration in 1916. In former years they had marched, not ridden, in parades. Their ranks were thinning, and in a few more years they would all have passed on.

Opposite: Circus parade on Mechanic Street, on its way to the show ground. The brick buildings in the right background had replaced earlier wooden ones shown on pages 88 and 89. The tower at the extreme right supports a bell. Some factories used such bells instead of whistles. One man who worked here shortly after World War I recalls that smoking was forbidden in the company buildings, and the bell tower was one place where the fellows went to sneak a smoke. If the bell rang when you weren't expecting it, the effect was startling.

Following pages: F. LaRiviere & Son, about 1898. LaRiviere was also one of the fire engineers, and the boys from the department used to patronize his place, which was almost next door to the firehouse.

Left: Three sisters. Patriotic celebrations received much attention, and children were often dressed up to take part in them.
Opposite: A parade, about 1920, on a rainy day on Main Street. The old elm trees were still on the edge of the roadway, on the left-hand side.
Below: Spanish-American War days, 1898. The unpaved roads were dusty, but that didn't bother the small boys.

Above: A group of Hamilton Woolen Company buildings, in the Globe. A load of hay, without its horses, stands near the tree in the foreground.

Opposite: A lumber mill and box shop (wooden boxes, of course).

Following pages: The Southbridge Print Works, in Sandersdale. The product was printed cloth. The stone wall at the bottom of the picture was part of the water-power canal. By this time, 1880, most factories used steam as well as water power, hence the tall chimneys.

85

Above: The American Optical Company's works on Mechanic Street.

Opposite, above: Another view of the American Optical Company, taken in 1882. The optical goods business was becoming one of the town's important industries.

Opposite, below: Work force. Note the ratio of men to women. The women probably did office work.

Above: The wool sorters of the Hamilton Woolen Company. Many of the men in this skilled occupation came from England.

Opposite: Globe Village seen from a cliff above the Quinebaug River, about 1880. The dam is the lower one of the Hamilton Woolen Company. Only a few of the company's factory buildings are visible. The dam of the "big pond" is out of sight beyond the factory building in the middle distance.

Following pages: Globe Village from a hill to the southwest, about 1880. Part of the Hamilton Woolen Company's "big pond" is in the foreground. The company's buildings occupy much of the left side of the picture. Cliff Street winds along the hill in back of them. (It was from a point on this street that the circular picture on the opposite page was taken.) The first Notre Dame Church of the French parish is at the upper center of the right side of the large picture. The steeple near the center of the left side is on the Free Evangelical Church, a nondenominational Protestant church. The building had been erected by the Hamilton Woolen Company to provide a church building for the group.

Above: The powerhouse crew at the American Optical Company, about 1921.

Opposite: The railroad line that never was: the Grand Trunk Line in construction through Southbridge, about 1910. The town never had a through railroad; its only line dead-ends here. This Grand Trunk project was intended to connect the area of Providence, R.I., with the Central Vermont Railroad at Palmer, Mass. (the Grand Trunk controlled the Central Vermont). Work stopped after the Grand Trunk president responsible for the project died in the sinking of the *Titanic* in 1912, and his successor chose not to continue it. The abandoned right-of-way can still be followed for miles across country. Many Italian men came here to work on the construction, and they and their families stayed on after work stopped.

Above: A friendly game.

Opposite: This gentleman had been a leader in the militia company which went from Southbridge to the Spanish-American War. In later years he sometimes gave patriotic talks in the schools. As often happens when children have to listen to their elders, not all the boys who heard the Major were favorably impressed. This shot dates from about 1898.

Opposite: Members of the infantry company, about 1889.
Right: A soldier in full uniform.

Above: Mother and child.
Opposite: A lady in her sitting room, about 1898.

Left: A young man and his prized pug, about 1889.

Opposite: Group on a summer's day. The women at the extreme right and left are dressed formally. The other woman must have just stepped out for the picture; she still has her apron on. The children are obediently docile.

Above: Family reunion at the old farm. The old gentleman's
ancestor had settled this farm in the 1730s or '40s, and it had
been in the family ever since. A companion picture, not
included here, shows the whole of the reunion group, some
thirty-odd sons, daughters, in-laws, grandchildren, nephews,
nieces and other relatives.
Opposite: Six young women on an outing.

A costume get-up for an entertainment. The "woman," of course, is a man.

This looks like the cast of a play, about 1898.

Above: The Law.
Opposite: Dandy and dog, about 1898.
Right: Dressed up for a play? The picture was taken
in 1898.

Traveling with horse and buggy, around 1898. This rig is
neat, clean and polished, and the horse looks well cared for.

Informal family portrait.

Left: A fireman of the "Tiger" company displays a hose nozzle. He is standing in front of the fire station shown on the opposite page.

Opposite: Combined fire and police stations, on Central Street, about 1880. The tower at the right was used for drying hoses. The fire station was here until a new building was put up on Elm Street in 1903. Then this building was converted to business uses.

113

Aaron Pease (*opposite*) and his laboratory (*above*). Mr. Pease was a photographer whose work was also his hobby. Among other things he liked to photograph sunsets with a variety of filters, although this was long before the days of color film. His porch gave a view to the west, and he had three holes drilled in the floor so that he could always set up his tripod in the same position. He is responsible for a number of the photographs in this book.

Wedding reception going-away picture, 1919. The reception had been held at the home of the bride's parents. The couple have changed from their wedding costumes to their traveling clothes and are ready to leave for the honeymoon trip. All the members of the two families pose with them. The ever-present humorous relative is at the left.

The Daughters of Union Veterans with the commander of
the G. A. R. post. His own daughter, in a light-colored dress,
is seated in front of him.

Girl in a goat cart, about 1898.

A stylish equipage.

Boy and dog, about 1898.

Boy and rooster—a picture from about 1898.

Most of these kids seem to have enjoyed posing for this picture.

These kids found that posing can be a serious matter, even when you are supposed to be having fun. The merry-go-round is equipped with a music box.

Left: The first-grade class at Notre Dame Convent parochial school, about 1896.

Above, upper: Studio photograph of George Gatineau (son of Felix) in the 1890s. His clothes were very much in fashion for the time. His seat and the backdrop were typical of studio props of the era.

Above, lower: Baby in basin.

Dressed up for a patriotic celebration, about 1898.

Group of children.

Above: Acrobat, about 1898. The bicycle was also a vehicle for displaying acrobatic prowess. Judging from the size of the rear hub, this one did not have a coaster brake.
Opposite: A group at the Y.

Left: The umbrella was used to avoid sunburn.

Opposite: Persis Rowley on the bridge in Westville. Not many women drove cars, at least if unaccompanied by a man; the effort to start the engine by hand-cranking was too great. The lady may simply have been posing for the picture. The lamps burned acetylene gas and had to be lighted with a match.

Below: Traveling entertainers of various sorts sometimes came to town.

The morning after the coon hunt. Except for the man with
the rifle, the fellows were probably wearing different clothes
the night before.

What is this group of middle-aged women? Why are several
of them holding dolls, and one a live cat? No one now seems
to know.

Opposite: A Valentine Ball in Edwards Hall at the top of the Edwards store building, about 1923.
Below: A trotting race at the annual Sturbridge Fair (strictly, the fair of the Worcester South Agricultural Society, covering the southern part of the county).

Above: A successful hunt in the "Breakneck" area of town.
Opposite: Another successful hunting expedition, but these
men have on their hunting clothes. Although two kerosene
lanterns are hanging from the posts, the middle man on the
porch is holding an electric lantern.

Left: Persis Rowley on snowshoes. Her sisters thought her brightly colored outfit quite loud, and called it "the Indian blanket." Today its pattern would be considered fairly quiet.

Opposite: Family reunion in the late 1880s. The elderly man in the left foreground had moved to town years before to play the organ in Saint Mary's Church, although he was himself a Church of England man and not a Roman Catholic. The church had acquired a new organ, but there was no one in town to play it. The Saint Mary's pastor heard of a man in neighboring Webster who could play and who might be induced to come to Southbridge if a job could be obtained for him in one of the mills. This was arranged. The man became a wool sorter for the Hamilton Woolen Company and played the Saint Mary's organ for many years. Some of his grandchildren, great-grandchildren and great-great-grandchildren still live in town.

Below: Skating on Number One Reservoir. Long skirts notwithstanding, the girls and women skated too.

One of Southbridge's early baseball teams. Many towns had
their own teams in those days.

A summer afternoon on the Quinebaug, about 1898.

Above: Another attraction at the Sturbridge Fair, this one in 1905. Many Southbridge men were active in the fair. After trolleys came, special cars were run to and from the fairgrounds, and they were loaded with passengers. Some old-timers say that in 1906 one of the Wright Brothers' planes was there and that Orville Wright himself was present, though another pilot flew the plane.

Opposite: An outing in the woods, about the time of the Spanish-American War, about 1898.

Above: Early Southbridge golfers.
Opposite: The first golfers' clubhouse, 1904 or 1905. The country club was later moved to another place, but there still is a Golf Street near the site shown here.

Left: Daredevil.
Opposite: Watermelon for dessert after the boys have a dinner at a summer cottage.

BLANCHARD'S
New Theatre.

Modern, Up-to-date, Ground Floor, Fireproof.

Playing the best of road attractions
High Class Vaudeville and
Motion Pictures.

OUR MOTTO:
"The best at all times at any price"

BLANCHARD BROTHERS
FRED. H.   SOL. E.   WILLIAM N.
ARTHUR A.   LOUIS L.

PROPRIETORS Blanchard's Theatre Building Block, COR. ELM AND MAIN STREETS, SOUTHBRIDGE, MASS.

6 — BLANCHARDS — 6

BLANCHARD'S SINGING ORCHESTRA,
SOUTHBRIDGE, MASS.

BLANCHARD FAMILY

6 — BLANCHARDS — 6

MUSIC FURNISHED FOR ALL OCCASIONS.
F. H. BLANCHARD, Director.   PROF. SOL. BLANCHARD, Prompter.
S. E. BLANCHARD, Manager.

Left, above: Card advertising the New Theatre.

Left: The Blanchards were leaders in the local field of popular music and entertainment, beginning in the 1890s. They organized a number of bands and orchestras, and went into the theater business. (One old resident who looked at these pictures mused, "The Blanchard boys; everybody liked 'em!")

Opposite: Interior of Blanchard's New Theatre, 1911. One of the orchestras furnished music for the films.

Above: The building at the southwest corner of Main and Elm Streets (the one with the Boston Branch sign in the title-page picture) has had several bad fires. This one in 1927 destroyed the Blanchard movie theater.

Opposite: The Strand Theater. The Strand was the last of the old movie houses. After it went out of business the town was without movies for several years until quite recently.

Following pages: An early car of the Southbridge & Sturbridge Street Railway. This open car was for summer use. The conductor walked along the running board to collect fares. At the end of the line the trolley pole would be pulled down and swung to the other end of the car, the reversible seat-backs flopped over, the fender at one end raised and the other lowered, and the car would be ready for the return trip.

Opposite: Main Street after a snowstorm, about 1898. Trolley cars arrived during the 1890s and soon became the principal means of transportation for many people. On one occasion, after several days of sleet and snow, the tracks were so frozen over that the plows could not clear them. Many people could not get to work. The mills closed, and the men and boys turned out with picks and shovels and worked until the tracks were open. Note the early movie posters.

Right: A ride in the four-seater, 1895. The whole family is present, from Father and two children in front to Grandpa and Grandma on the back seat. This vehicle is equipped with brakes, which work against the iron tires of the rear wheels.

Below: At the depot, leaving for an excursion.

Above: Funeral of one of the town's leading industrialists, 1912. The pomp is in contrast to the simplicity of the burial on the opposite page.

Opposite: An Albanian goes to his grave far from the place of his birth, although the priest is clad as he would be in the old country. Picture taken in 1924.

Above: A parlor, with a glimpse of the grand piano and a
view into the dining room and the front hall.
Opposite: Elaborate ornamentation of house fronts was in
style for a time. This shot is probably from about 1900.

Interior of a summer cottage.

A summer dwelling on the shore of a pond near Southbridge.

The Ellis-Merritt house (*opposite*) and a family group on its porch (*above*). Today this would be called a duplex. The near side was occupied by the Merritt family, the farther by the Ellises.

Above: The Bank Building, housing both the Southbridge National Bank and the Southbridge Savings Bank, about 1890. Most New England villages of any pretensions had an ornamental watering trough. The one from which the horse is drinking is surmounted by an oil lamp.

Opposite: Saint Mary's Church, Roman Catholic. The original single parish was divided in 1870, one part being French and the other mainly Irish. This is the church of the second group.

Above: The home of the owner of a local knife factory. (The steeple of the Universalist Church shows in the background.) There were four competing cutlery factories in town, two of them owned and operated by descendants of Henry Harrington, a local inventor and craftsman who began his business about the time Southbridge was incorporated.

Opposite: The Universalist Church, on the corner of Main and Hamilton Streets, built in 1841. The graceful steeple blew down in a hurricane in 1938 and was never rebuilt. A few years ago the Universalists, one of the first denominations in town, disbanded and the building was sold. It now houses several offices and stores.

SOURCES OF THE PICTURES

Most of the photographs come from four collections. The others were loaned by a number of individuals. The collections are as follows.

1. An album, "Southbridge Illustrated," photographer not named, published by Lithograph Printing Co., 115 Nassau Street, New York. It is undated, but from evidence in the pictures the time was about 1880. An incomplete copy is in the Jacob Edwards Memorial Library, Southbridge. Another copy was loaned by Mr. Ernest Peloquin.

2. A collection of mounted photographs, stamped on the back: "From C. E. Hill, Jewelry and Music Store, Southbridge, Mass." According to penciled notes on each, they were taken in July 1889. They were taken by Mr. Hill, and were probably part of a large collection possessed by his widow, who survived him by many years. She sold parts of the collection to vari-

ous persons. Most of the pictures appearing here belong to the Southbridge Historical Society. A few more are from a group recently donated to the Jacob Edwards Library.

3. A large collection of photographs by Aaron H. Pease, a Southbridge photographer from the 1890s until the 1930s. Most of the collection consists of a set of albums and some loose pictures in the possession of Mr. W. C. Eaton. A smaller number of pictures are owned by the Southbridge Historical Society.

4. The Tucci Collection. Mr. George Tucci was an avid collector of pictures of the town, both antique and contemporary, for many years. He has presented his collection to the Jacob Edwards Library.

Numbering of the photographs indicates the pages on which they appear.

SOURCES OF PICTURES

74–75. A. H. Pease
78. Courtesy W. C. Eaton
79. A. H. Pease
80–81. A. H. Pease
82. (bottom) A. H. Pease
86–87. "Southbridge Illustrated"
88. Tucci Collection
89. (top) Courtesy W. C. Eaton
89. (bottom) Courtesy Southbridge Historical Society
90. "Southbridge Illustrated"
91. Courtesy John Crosbie
92–93. "Southbridge Illustrated"
94. A. H. Pease
96. A. H. Pease
97. A. H. Pease
98. A. H. Pease
99. A. H. Pease
100. A. H. Pease
102. A. H. Pease
104. Courtesy Fred Sibley
105. Probably photographed by A. H. Pease. Courtesy Southbridge Historical Society
106. Courtesy Lionel Peloquin
107. A. H. Pease
108. A. H. Pease
109. (left) Courtesy Southbridge Historical Society
109. (right) A. H. Pease
110. A. H. Pease
112. A. H. Pease
113. "Southbridge Illustrated"
114. Courtesy Southbridge Historical Society
115. A. H. Pease
116. Courtesy Lionel Peloquin
118. A. H. Pease
120. A. H. Pease
121. A. H. Pease
122. A. H. Pease
123. Courtesy Southbridge Historical Society
124–25. Courtesy Lionel Peloquin
125. (top) Courtesy George Gatineau
125. (bottom) A. H. Pease
126. A. H. Pease
127. A. H. Pease
128. A. H. Pease
129. Courtesy Fred Sibley
131. Courtesy Fred Sibley
134. Photograph by A. H. Pease in Tucci Collection
135. Courtesy John J. O'Shaughnessy
136. Courtesy Roland J. Meunier
137. Courtesy Lionel Peloquin
138. (top) Courtesy Fred Sibley
138–39. Courtesy Fred Sibley
139. (top) Courtesy John Crosbie
140. Courtesy Roland J. Meunier
141. A. H. Pease
142. A. H. Pease
143. A. H. Pease
144. A. H. Pease
145. A. H. Pease
147. A. H. Pease
148. (bottom) Courtesy Worcester Evening Gazette
149. Courtesy Southbridge Historical Society
150. A. H. Pease
152–53. Tucci Collection
154. A. H. Pease
155. (top) Courtesy John J. O'Shaughnessy
156. A. H. Pease
157. Courtesy Southbridge Historical Society
158. Photograph by Lovell in Tucci Collection
159. Courtesy Southbridge Historical Society
160. A. H. Pease
161. A. H. Pease
162. Courtesy W. C. Eaton
163. Courtesy W. C. Eaton